SANDI TOKSVIG

Born in Copenhagen, Sandi Toksvig is a well-known broadcaster and writer. She began her comedy career at Girton College, Cambridge University, where she wrote and performed in the first all-female show for the Cambridge Footlights. She performed at the first night of The Comedy Store in London and was part of the famous improvisational comedy team, The Comedy Store Players.

Sandi has appeared on a variety of television programmes including *No 73*, *Whose Line Is It Anyway?*, *Call My Bluff*, *QI*, *Playhouse Live* and *1001 Things You Should Know*. She is a familiar voice for Radio 4 listeners, as the chair of *The News Quiz*, and was the main presenter of its travel programme *Excess Baggage* until 2012.

Sandi's work for the theatre includes *Bully Boy*, a musical *Big Night Out at the Little Palace Theatre* and *Pocket Dream*. She has written books for both adults and children, which include *Girls Are Best*, *Hitler's Canary*, *The Chain of Curiosity* and her latest novel *Valentine Grey*.

Sandi became the chancellor of Portsmouth University in January 2012.

Other Titles in this Series

Sandi Toksvig

BULLY BOY

NICK HERN BOOKS

London

www.nickhernbooks.co.uk

A Nick Hern Book

Bully Boy first published in 2012 by Nick Hern Books Limited, The Glasshouse, 49a Goldhawk Road, London W12 8QP

Bully Boy copyright © 2012 Sandi Toksvig

Sandi Toksvig has asserted her right to be identified as the author of this work

Cover image: Dewynters
Cover design: Ned Hoste, 2H

Typeset by Nick Hern Books, London
Printed and bound in Great Britain by Mimeo Ltd, Huntingdon, Cambridgeshire PE29 6XX

A CIP catalogue record for this book is available from the British Library

ISBN 978 1 84842 296 4

Woodland
CARBON
www.woodlandcarbon.co.uk
NICK HERN BOOKS
Printed on Carbon Captured paper

Introduction

For someone who thinks of themselves as a pacifist I have
written a lot about war lately. Perhaps it is not so surprising. We
are all subjected to images of conflict every day as one faction or
another shoots it out in Syria or Iraq or Afghanistan or Sudan or
any number of other distant places which come home to us
through the television. At first my interest was mostly academic.
I was working on my new novel, *Valentine Grey*. It concerns a
young Victorian woman who, in 1899, decides to escape the
confines of the drawing room by disguising herself as a man and
going to serve in the second Anglo-Boer War. The war is
interesting on many fronts, not least the fact that it was one of
the first where the average soldier was literate. As a
consequence, there are many contemporary diaries and I found I
was able to march with the men as they battled across the veld.
The stories were personal as some began to question what they
were doing so many miles from home. As I studied the conflict, I
realised that the war was not about morals or freedom but about
money and influence, and it made me think how little has
changed.

The Honourable Artillery Company in London provided
many Boer War volunteers and my research there led to my
being invited to a regimental dinner. As I sat chatting with
soldiers serving today, my thinking turned from whole regiments
in battle to individuals. Meanwhile, my partner, a
psychotherapist, was dealing with a number of returned veterans
in a private mental-health facility. She was enraged by their
treatment and came home each day in a state of distress.

I began to read about the effect of war on the individual. In
particular, Dave Grossman's book *On Killing: The
Psychological Cost of Learning to Kill in War and Society*,
which had a huge effect on me. Some of the facts were
astonishing. In Vietnam, it took an average of 50,000 rounds of
ammunition to kill one enemy soldier. The truth is if the
Americans had really wanted to be efficient on the battlefield,

they would have been better off with bows and arrows. The US troops, it seems, were reluctant to kill anyone, and when they returned home anywhere between 400,000 and 1.5 million veterans of that war suffered from post-traumatic stress disorder. I read about every war's legacy amongst combatants of all nations – divorce, marital problems, tranquiliser use, alcoholism, joblessness, heart disease, high blood pressure, ulcers and of course, tragically, suicide.

I was already appalled by the Bush/Cheney strategy of 'All-them-ragheads-look-alike-to-me' which conflated 9/11 and Iraq; of the average member of the public's inability to distinguish between Afghanistan and Iraq, and my rage grew. I thought about the young men I had met who had been sent to do an incomprehensibly difficult job by their nation and who, in many instances, had not been cared for properly when they returned home, broken inside. I wondered where the movies might be which celebrate the returning veteran and yet explain his vulnerable emotional state? I had so many questions. How is it possible that one in ten prisoners in England and Wales once served in the armed forces? What has gone wrong that half of all GPs are unaware of official guidelines on how to diagnose mental-health trauma because of battle scars from the front line?

When Patrick Sandford, artistic director of the Nuffield Theatre in Southampton, said he wanted to commission a play from me it was as if *Bully Boy* poured out of my head. Part of the problem with an issue as complex and distressing as soldiers' mental health is getting people to engage with it. I have always believed that the theatre is a wonderful forum for confronting difficult subjects. 'Theatre' comes from the Greek word 'theatron' meaning 'place for seeing'. It is a communal place where we come together for an exchange of ideas; where we can explore experiences which may have nothing to do with our daily lives but which touch our humanity.

There is much more to say than can be covered in a single play. In the end, I focused on a tale of just two men, but I am not unaware of the stories that remain untold. The truth is most Iraqi children now suffer from psychological symptoms. According to a study of 10,000 primary-school students in the Shaab section of North Baghdad, seventy per cent of children are suffering from trauma-related issues.

I remain full of rage on behalf of the young men who have been sent to do older men's political bidding. I am appalled that George Bush and Tony Blair colluded in misinformation to the public. Bush quit drinking – it would have been better if he had quit lying. Meanwhile, Tony Blair ended up fantastically rich and, irony of ironies, a peace envoy.

I am thrilled to have penned this piece for Southampton, and that it has gone on to a new life in Northampton and become the opening production at the new St. James Theatre in London. North, south, I need people to pay attention – not to me but to the men whose voices deserve to be heard.

Sandi Toksvig
August 2012

Bully Boy was first performed at the Nuffield Theatre, Southampton, on 13 May 2011 (previews from 10 May). The cast was as follows:

OSCAR	Anthony Andrews
EDDIE	Joshua Miles
Director	Patrick Sandford
Dramaturg	Pip Broughton

The play was revived in a new production first performed at the Royal & Derngate, Northampton, on 24 August 2012, before transferring to the St. James Theatre, London, on 18 September 2012. The cast was as follows:

OSCAR	Anthony Andrews
EDDIE	Joshua Miles
Directors	Patrick Sandford, David Gilmore
Designer	Simon Higlett
Lighting Designer	James Whiteside
Sound Designer	John Leonard

It was produced by St. James Theatre Productions in association with Lee Dean, Charles Diamond, Daniel Schumann and Royal & Derngate, Northampton.

Characters

OSCAR
EDDIE

This text went to press before the end of rehearsals and so may differ slightly from the play as performed.

Prologue

The stage is dark. Only OSCAR, *a senior officer, can be seen. He stands and addresses the audience. He is very well spoken although at first he is somewhat hesitant.*

OSCAR. Major Oscar Hadley… I was the officer in charge of the investigation. I am grateful for the chance to appear… I have some things to say.

I've been reading… about the Battle of Gettysburg. I can assure you this is relevant. It took place, as I'm certain you know, in 1863, and it was the turning point of the American Civil War.

One hundred and fifty thousand men fought and after the battle was over the muskets, it's a valuable gun, which had been abandoned on the field were recovered. There was more than twenty-seven thousand of them and here is the curious thing – nearly ninety per cent of the guns on the ground after the battle were found to be fully loaded, ready to fire but had not actually been discharged.

Many of them, half, had been loaded more than once. Loading was quite complicated… it took a long time… so the question is – can that many soldiers have been mistaken about the state of their gun? Surely if someone is shooting at you, then the first thing you do, once you are ready, is to shoot back?

Why were there so many unfired guns? What were they worried about? Shooting a countryman? Killing a brother?

Well, maybe the soldiers kept loading because they wanted to look as though they were doing what was required. As if they were fighting when they actually weren't. Maybe they simply didn't want to kill anyone. Maybe most people, even soldiers, don't want to kill anyone.

Which brings me to Private Edward Clark…

Scene One

We see the stage for the first time. It is bare save for a table and chair. The sounds of guns firing can be heard mixed with occasional explosions and a helicopter taking off. EDDIE, a young soldier of twenty, runs in. He is from Burnley in Lancashire. A fit-looking fellow, he is clearly in a very agitated state. He tries to calm himself down. He removes an iPhone from his pocket and begins playing a war game on it. He mutters to himself as the game progresses and cannot keep still.

OSCAR *enters in a wheelchair carrying a briefcase. EDDIE does not notice him and carries on playing. OSCAR sits patiently looking at the young man.*

OSCAR. You winning?

EDDIE. Yeah. (*Carries on playing.*) You waiting for the monkey?

OSCAR. Not really. I am the monkey.

> EDDIE *immediately stops playing the game and stands to attention.*

EDDIE. Sorry, sir. I was just… been trying to… it's all been a bit… sorry.

> *The sound of warfare continues from the small games console.*

OSCAR. The game?

EDDIE. Yes, sir. Sorry, sir.

> EDDIE *fumbles with the game and turns it off. The war sounds finish.*

OSCAR. That's better.

EDDIE. They didn't tell me, sir.

OSCAR. Tell you what?

EDDIE. That you were… (*Eyeing the wheelchair.*) Nothing, sir.

OSCAR. They didn't tell you nothing. What an excellent start. It means we can begin from my preferred place, the beginning.

EDDIE. I didn't mean monkey, I meant…

OSCAR. Yes. Sit down. I am Major Hadley from…

EDDIE. Special Investigations… I know, they told me.

OSCAR. And you are…

> OSCAR *checks a piece of paper.*

> Private Edward Clark.

EDDIE. Yes, sir. Eddie. They call me Eddie.

OSCAR. Indeed.

> OSCAR *continues to look at his paperwork.*

EDDIE. Have you flown out specially from back home?

OSCAR. Yes.

EDDIE. Sir?

OSCAR. Yes?

EDDIE. Do I have to sit, sir?

OSCAR. No. No, I suppose not.

> EDDIE *gets to his feet. He is restless.*

EDDIE. How did you get the chair. Wheelchair?

OSCAR. I served in the Falklands.

EDDIE. Right. Major, I need to know, is it about the boy or the whole thing? Somebody said…

OSCAR. What do you think it should be about?

EDDIE. I just wondered… am I under arrest?

OSCAR. Do you think you should be?

EDDIE. I'm sorry but are you going to do that the whole time?

OSCAR. I beg your pardon?

EDDIE. The whole time… sir?

OSCAR. Do what?

EDDIE. Ask questions instead of answering. It's just they brought me straight here and I don't even…

OSCAR. It's my job to ask questions. I'm here to try and sort out what happened. That's what I do.

EDDIE. That's what I'm asking – is it about the boy or the whole thing?

OSCAR. How old are you, Eddie?

EDDIE. Twenty, sir.

OSCAR. Been in the army a long time?

EDDIE. Four years.

OSCAR. From…

EDDIE. Sixteen, sir.

OSCAR. Yes, yes, I can do the arithmetic, Clark. The town, what town are you from?

EDDIE. Burnley, Lancashire.

OSCAR. Burnley. What does that mean? Burnley?

EDDIE. Mean, sir. What do you mean, what does it mean?

OSCAR. The name. What does the name mean? Everything means something.

EDDIE. I have no idea.

OSCAR. Never been curious to find out?

EDDIE. No, sir.

OSCAR. Lived there all your life?

EDDIE. Till the army.

OSCAR. Any qualifications?

EDDIE. I can drive.

OSCAR. You can drive. That it?

EDDIE. Uhm, you mean GCSEs?

OSCAR. That sort of thing.

EDDIE. No, sir.

OSCAR. Well done, Burnley. 'Education, education, education.'

EDDIE. Not a big reader.

OSCAR. You should try it some time. Might surprise yourself.

EDDIE. You like books?

OSCAR. Yes I do. They inform you. Make you feel everything is knowable and if things are knowable, well then, like Adam in Paradise naming the animals, you can command them.

OSCAR *feels he has given too much away.*

EDDIE. We used to call that being a nerd.

OSCAR. Indeed. Major Nerd.

EDDIE. I'm sorry but no one will tell me. The sarge?

OSCAR. Sergeant Payne? He was air-lifted out this morning. We shall have to wait and see. I'm sorry.

OSCAR *takes a moment to let the news register.*

Now, you know how this works and I am sure you will want to make it right, for the sergeant's sake. You've been with him a long time.

EDDIE. Six months.

OSCAR. Quite the little unit. I gather you call yourselves 'The Bully Boys'.

EDDIE. Not really. I mean yes but it didn't mean anything. That's Jack.

OSCAR. Jack McNeil?

EDDIE. He's always saying 'Bully for you' if you win something or do something and we all started saying it. You know what Jack's like.

OSCAR. Not really.

EDDIE. He likes a laugh. He's Irish. He's funny. You'd need to be with that hair. (*Awkward*.) He's ginger. Anyway, it sort of stuck. Bully Boy. It's nothing.

OSCAR. I need to know what happened.

EDDIE. You know what happened.

OSCAR. Let's start with Omar.

EDDIE. Omar? Who the fuck is Omar?

OSCAR. The boy. He was called Omar. I just thought you'd like to know, that was his name.

EDDIE. I didn't know, did I? It's not like we were making fucking friends.

OSCAR. When did you first see him?

EDDIE. Sorry?

OSCAR. The boy.

EDDIE. Sergeant Payne might die and you want to talk about one boy? One bastard raghead? We could all be dead. I got nothing to say. Do I have to do this? I don't have to do this.

OSCAR *gets ready to leave*.

OSCAR. No you don't have to. Shame though. You are last on my list. I've spoken to the others. I would have liked to have got your version.

EDDIE. Version? What do you mean, version? What does that mean?

OSCAR. These are difficult situations. I'm sure there was a lot of confusion.

EDDIE *laughs as if* OSCAR *can have no idea*.

It's my job to try and get the full picture. We have given the local people an undertaking to find out what happened.

EDDIE. Sand niggers.

OSCAR. Private Clark, I am going to have to ask you to refrain from that kind of language.

EDDIE. What do you want to call them? Camel jockeys? You want me to worry about the locals? It's 'the target'. They don't worry about me.

OSCAR. And it helps you to dehumanise them by calling them names?

EDDIE. Why can't you talk English? Look, you keep telling me you've got a job to do. So have I. If locals get killed that's 'collateral damage', isn't that right? I can't help that.

OSCAR. Unless, of course, you deliberately throw a boy down a well. Then that's murder.

EDDIE *stops pacing and there is a pause as they look at each other.*

The others say you were closest. You were closest to the boy.

EDDIE. Who said that?

OSCAR. They say you were closest to the boy when he was last seen.

EDDIE. Jack wouldn't say that. He didn't say that. Brian? Was it Brian?

OSCAR. Let's be very clear here, Clark, you don't have to tell me anything. The others have already given a very detailed description but it will go easier if you cooperate.

EDDIE. I have nothing to say.

OSCAR. An eight-year-old boy is dead. Thrown down a well. How big was he? About this tall? Skinny, little fella? Hardly a fight for a man, was it? For a man from Burnley. What did you do? Pick him up with one hand? Did he cry out? Omar? Did he cry all the way down until the water splashed over him and he drowned or did he hit his head on the way and fall silently into the dark?

EDDIE *stands to attention and doesn't speak.*

Very well. You will be confined to quarters until further notice. That will be all.

Scene Two

OSCAR *is sitting in his chair, looking at something on the floor with fascination.* EDDIE *comes in and salutes. He is clearly agitated.* OSCAR *does not look at him.*

OSCAR. Clark, you are returned.

EDDIE. I asked to speak to you. A guard… he brought me over. The others? Are they…?

OSCAR *continues to look at the table.*

What you doing?

OSCAR. There's a spider just there.

EDDIE. A spider?

OSCAR. Never seen one like it.

EDDIE *looks to where* OSCAR *points and then grinds the spot with his foot.* OSCAR *looks up at him.*

Are the others what?

EDDIE. Are they confined to quarters? I haven't seen anyone. I don't really know what's happening.

OSCAR. Do you know I sometimes think my job is like interviewing a group of blind men who have groped an elephant?

EDDIE *stands bemused.*

One blind man has grasped what he thinks is a tree, another has found a wall, still another discovered a snake – all of them have a piece of the puzzle, a piece of the truth.

EDDIE. I don't know what you're talking about.

OSCAR. No. I heard about Sergeant Payne. I'm sorry. I thought he'd make it but there we are. Is that why you decided to speak? I gather you have something to say.

EDDIE. They won't let me see the others.

OSCAR. We need to get to the facts. I don't want their stories clouding yours.

EDDIE. I need to talk to them. I want to know what they told you.

OSCAR *looks at him and removes a gun from his briefcase.*

OSCAR. I have your weapons.

EDDIE. Lot of use they're going to be to you.

OSCAR. You didn't fire them.

EDDIE. I were a bit busy.

OSCAR. You were being shot at, yet you didn't fire your gun.

EDDIE. There was shooting everywhere. Plenty of people were shooting.

OSCAR. So I gather. How long have you been at the front, Eddie?

EDDIE. At the front? There is no fucking front. It's not the bloody Second World War. There is no front. There's no line where you know the fighting is going on. If there was there'd be some place you could be safe, right? But there's nowhere. Haven't you heard? It's 'an insurgency'. Do you get that? It means it's everywhere. When I kit up I have no idea who wants to kill me or why. There is no front line. There's never going to be some victory where we march into the capital and raise up our flag while some fucking band plays.

OSCAR. You seem very agitated.

EDDIE. I can't think why. Sergeant Payne is dead. I save me fucking unit and now I'm under a fucking, shiting, pointless, pigging investigation.

OSCAR. This is your second deployment?

EDDIE. Yes.

OSCAR. How long have you got left?

EDDIE. A month. If they let me stay. Look, I want to have my say. I don't want you to just hear it from them. I know what happened – a boy with a grenade tried to kill me.

OSCAR. Is that what you think?

EDDIE. Not me… us. It's what I know. It's not fair if you just hear it from the others.

OSCAR. Brian… uhm…

EDDIE. Robinson. What did he say? He wouldn't say anything. Not Brian.

OSCAR. He said there were six of you near the well.

EDDIE. Yes. Brian, Sergeant Payne, Jack, Paki, Harley…

OSCAR. Paki?

EDDIE. You know, what's his name, Hakim.

OSCAR. Paki? I thought he was Malaysian?

EDDIE. He's not bothered. He looks Paki but it don't matter. Harley's a Welsh bastard. We don't care.

OSCAR. What are they like?

EDDIE. What do you mean?

OSCAR. Brian. Is he quiet, serious, a laugh like, uhmm… Jack?

EDDIE. I don't know. He's… solid.

OSCAR. Solid?

EDDIE. Got your back has Brian. Built like a brick shithouse.

OSCAR. And what's Harley like?

EDDIE. Why do you keep asking what people are like? You've met them. What does it matter?

OSCAR. I'm trying to get a picture of you all. A picture of what happened. Harley?

EDDIE. I don't bloody know. He's small. Smaller than me. He's a bloke. A Welsh bloke. He likes music. Fucking loud singing, alright? Harley likes singing, Jack's a laugh, Brian's

a fit bastard and Hakim is like a fucking local with a
Cockney accent, alright?

OSCAR. And you were all behind the well?

EDDIE. Yes.

OSCAR. Why?

EDDIE (*sighs*). It was that woman. That woman. She wanted to
kill us.

OSCAR. What woman?

EDDIE. The one in the square. She were just standing there.
Didn't have a gun or nothing. Maybe she was his mother. I
don't know. Nobody wanted to kill her. She was somebody's
mother. You don't kill somebody's mother but you know
what she was doing? Turning to face us whenever we moved
so the other sand niggers could see where we were. She was
like a fucking rifle sight for them.

OSCAR. How did you know that? How did you know that's
what she was doing?

EDDIE. I didn't. Sergeant Payne... I know they're saying bad
things about him but I'm not having it. He looked out for us.
He saw it. There wasn't supposed to be trouble there. We'd
been through the village before. The woman gave us food.

OSCAR. Which woman?

EDDIE. The same woman. She gave us bread. We thought it
was okay. It just kicked off from nothing. It had been quiet
and then there was shooting everywhere and she kept giving
us away.

OSCAR. Are you sure?

EDDIE. She kept turning one way and then the other.

OSCAR. Perhaps she was just looking for her boy. Is that
possible?

EDDIE. You're trying to make this worse than it was.

OSCAR. Then what happened?

EDDIE. Sarge kept shouting to Harley coz he had the best shot but he didn't hear.

OSCAR. Why not?

EDDIE. His iPod.

OSCAR. What do you mean, his iPod?

EDDIE. He listens to his iPod. I told you – singing.

OSCAR. You are joking?

EDDIE. Anyway he couldn't hold his gun. Kept shaking. He's not been right and I have said but no one listens. He wasn't right then. That's why we put him down behind the well. That's why we were there. So the sarge stood up to take the woman out and got one right in the stomach. Then Paki fired at the woman and...

OSCAR. And what?

EDDIE. And he got her and she looked right at him, looked right at him before she fell. Then he pissed himself and he was making these funny noises... like he couldn't breathe. I thought he'd been hit. Jack and Brian were trying to sort the sarge, he were bleeding everywhere, so there wasn't anyone else. I was trying to organise us. There were no one else to organise us.

OSCAR. And the boy?

EDDIE. He came out of nowhere and Brian shouted 'grenade'. Everyone was yelling and there were shots and I thought I could hear singing really far away but then I noticed Harley's headphones had fallen off. Suddenly the boy was there and the sarge is bleeding everywhere and the next thing you know the kid is down the well.

OSCAR. How? How did he get down the well?

EDDIE. I don't know.

OSCAR. You don't know? You were there.

EDDIE. I don't remember. Did I have my hat on when we met?

OSCAR. What?

EDDIE. My hat. Was I wearing my hat when we met?

OSCAR. I don't know. I've no idea.

EDDIE. No. You don't remember. No one was firing at you and you still can't remember.

OSCAR. This isn't about hats. You just told me you were in charge. The others say it was you.

EDDIE. No. No they don't. We're in it together.

OSCAR. They say you picked him up and threw him in.

EDDIE. No! We're a team. We do everything together.

OSCAR. But you didn't do everything together. You never fired your gun.

EDDIE. What are you saying? If I had shot him that would be okay?

OSCAR. You threw an eight-year-old boy down a well.

EDDIE. I didn't say that. He was going to kill us. She was going to get us killed.

OSCAR. But it is possible that the dead woman was simply looking for her son and he was looking for her?

EDDIE (*less confident*). He was a raghead. A raghead with a fucking grenade.

OSCAR. He was eight years old.

EDDIE. Doesn't mean he didn't want to kill me.

OSCAR. So it was you.

EDDIE. I didn't say that. I never said that.

OSCAR. Eddie, the boy's body has been recovered. There was no grenade.

There is a blackout followed by the sound of an explosion and a flash of white light.

Scene Three

OSCAR *is sitting in his chair, staring out at the audience.*

EDDIE *enters behind* OSCAR *and stops for a minute to look at him before speaking.*

EDDIE. Hello… sir.

> OSCAR *doesn't react.* EDDIE *slowly moves round so that* OSCAR *can see him. Throughout,* OSCAR *is very disconnected due to the pain relief he is on.*

It's me, sir, Clark, Eddie Clark.

OSCAR. Clark. Are you alright?

EDDIE. Not a mark on me. The padre says it's a miracle.

> *Pause.*

He's a tosser. Sorry, sir.

OSCAR. I'm not dressed.

EDDIE. No. That's okay. They said it was alright… I asked. I just wanted to know.

OSCAR. I don't have my uniform.

EDDIE. Look, they told me what you're doing out here, what you were doing.

OSCAR. I'm sorry, I can't hear you.

EDDIE. It wasn't just the boy, was it? That's not why you came. Why didn't you tell me? It was Sergeant Payne and the lads, everything but you have to leave it now. Now, you have to leave it alone.

OSCAR. My ears.

EDDIE. Your hearing. The nurse told me. Said it would go. Not permanent, but I need to know.

OSCAR. I don't remember.

EDDIE. There was an explosion. The vehicle? You were taking us back to base from the village. The lads were… were in the other truck. Don't you remember? The bang? I pulled you out. They brought you here.

OSCAR. Sit.

EDDIE *takes his time getting a chair and sitting down.*

Has my mother called?

EDDIE. Your mother? I don't know. I could ask.

OSCAR. She'll call. She always calls.

EDDIE. Did you need anything? Fags? I don't know. Pain? You in pain?

OSCAR. They give me morphine.

EDDIE. Nice.

OSCAR. Morphine is nice but I can't hear properly so I can't… dance. I can't dance.

EDDIE. No. Sorry.

OSCAR. I am a helluva dancer.

EDDIE. Right.

OSCAR. Anything – soft-shoe, ballroom, Latin American. My mother taught me. She taught everyone but I was the best. She'll be cross because now I can't dance at all.

EDDIE. No.

OSCAR. Because I can't hear. Can't hear the music.

EDDIE *sits, not knowing what to say.*

EDDIE. No.

OSCAR. My mother's probably working.

EDDIE. I wanted to talk to you. After this – you'll leave it alone now, won't you?

OSCAR. I don't really know what you are saying.

EDDIE. No.

Scene Four

EDDIE *and* OSCAR *are seated side by side. The sound of engines indicate that they are on a plane heading home. The men are not speaking.*

There is the sound of take-off and then the engine noise fades. EDDIE *takes out his games console and turns it on. The sound of a war game begins.*

OSCAR. Could you turn that fucking thing off?

EDDIE. Sorry. Yes, sir. (*Turns it off.*) Didn't think you could hear it.

OSCAR. There is nothing wrong with my hearing.

EDDIE. No.

OSCAR. I am fine.

EDDIE. So you said.

OSCAR. It was entirely temporary.

There is a long silence.

EDDIE. Shouldn't you be at the front?

OSCAR. The front?

EDDIE. Of the plane. First class.

OSCAR. There is no fucking front.

EDDIE. Don't suppose there'll be a film.

OSCAR. Military transport are not usually big on entertainment.

EDDIE. Went to Florida once. Disneyland. With my granddad. I were eight. We had a film. Can't think what it was but it were nice – having a film on a plane. Flying.

EDDIE *shuts his eyes and settles down to sleep.* OSCAR *gets out a large book.*

Scene Four B

Apart from OSCAR*'s reading light above his seat, it is dark.*
EDDIE *awakes with a cry.*

EDDIE. No. No.

> EDDIE *struggles to get out of his seat.* OSCAR *tries to help him to sit down again.* EDDIE *is crying.*

OSCAR. It's alright, Clark, it's alright. Have some water.

> OSCAR *gives* EDDIE *some water from a bottle, which he gulps down. They are both embarrassed.*

EDDIE. I'm fine. Sorry.

OSCAR. That's okay.

> EDDIE *takes a deep sigh and wipes his face. The men sit in uncomfortable silence.*

EDDIE. Sleeping is shit.

OSCAR. Sometimes.

EDDIE. I can't stop thinking about it. You don't remember, do you? Wish I'd had a blow to the head.

OSCAR. I read the report.

EDDIE. You were so determined I wouldn't speak to the lads. I should have been with them. You made me go with you in the vehicle in front. We were moving so slow. Just been through the checkpoint. I'd been sitting next to you. The convoy got held up. I don't know what. Goats. Fucking goats or something. You let me get out. Check ahead.

OSCAR. Look, Clark... I'm trying to read.

EDDIE. People talk about explosions but you don't know, do you? Not really? Everything went white. Knocked the shit out of me. Improvised Explosive Device, my arse. They're getting better and better. Vehicle landed on its side and you were out cold. I knew you couldn't get out even if you woke. You were taking us back to base. The others were in the vehicle behind. Brian, Jack, Paki, Harley. My mates. The Bully Boys. I thought they were my mates but you said they told you about the boy. Said I killed him. After all we'd been through. I was angry with them. I don't want to be angry with them... not now...

The blast took half the road with it. Funny thing is, their vehicle looked fine. Honestly. Just the same as before. I ran to the back to open up. Get them out. I thought they were alright because there was no noise. I couldn't hear any noise from inside but you know, shock, maybe they were shocked. I couldn't get the doors open. I was pulling at them. The handle was hot. Then the doors burst open. It was the liquid, you see. Like a fire hose of hot liquid exploding over me. There was nothing but liquid. Just liquid. Hot liquid where the lads had been and it drenched me. My friends poured over me. The smell.

There is an uncomfortable silence.

OSCAR. Is someone coming to meet you?

EDDIE. Me dad.

OSCAR. Your mother?

EDDIE. No. She doesn't travel. Went to Manchester once. Didn't like it. Suzanne might come.

OSCAR. Suzanne?

EDDIE. Girlfriend. Works at Greggs the bakers. Serving. That's how we met. I get free sausage rolls. She'll probably be working.

There is a long pause.

I can't stop thinking about them. In the back of the plane except not really. Not really there. Just an empty box. Boxes. Four boxes.

OSCAR. It's for the families.

EDDIE. Will they know?

OSCAR. No.

EDDIE. Good. We flew out together. Me and the lads. Flew out on the same plane. (*There is a long silence.*) It were *Saving Private Ryan*.

OSCAR. What was?

EDDIE. The film on the plane to Disneyland. Funny that.

Scene Five

Military music is playing. EDDIE *is standing to attention.* OSCAR *is saluting. As the music fades,* EDDIE *moves away for a moment and then returns.*

OSCAR. Was that your father?

EDDIE. Yes.

OSCAR. What does he do?

EDDIE. Drinks mostly.

OSCAR. He must be pleased to see you.

EDDIE. He has no idea. Just shook me by the hand and said 'Hello, Eddie,' like I'd been out for a packet of fags.

OSCAR. I'd better have a word with the families. Look, don't call Hakim 'Paki' to his mother, will you? You coming?

EDDIE. Can't. Jack's mum keeps crying. I can't.

OSCAR. I'm sure they'd like to see you.

EDDIE *shakes his head.*

Right. Well, I'll be in touch.

EDDIE. Be in touch?

OSCAR. Mind how you go.

OSCAR *wheels away, leaving* EDDIE *standing alone. A phone rings.* EDDIE *can't think what the noise is and then realises it is his own phone ringing in his pocket. He removes it slowly and looks at it for a moment before answering.*

EDDIE. Hello? Hello, Suzanne. Yes. How am I?

EDDIE *does not know the answer to the question. He looks at the phone and then hangs up.*

Scene Six

OSCAR *is standing and continuing his opening speech to the audience.*

OSCAR. Although the investigation was ongoing, Private Clark was given compassionate leave to go home. Burnley in Lancashire. Near Pendle Hill. I didn't see him for some weeks. My hearing troubled me and I had several other cases that were ongoing. I was busy. I'm always busy. Then he came to see me. He was very angry. I think something had happened at home. He'd been arrested for hitting a girl. I don't really know how it happened but when he came to see me things got out of hand. I should have called the Military Police but I didn't. He left.

The next thing I heard was that he had gone missing. The police caught him running on the top of a moving train. Imagine that. Running on the top of a train. It was crazy. I mean, it seemed crazy.

OSCAR *falters for a moment.*

Sorry, I... do you mind if I sit down?

He sits.

Crazy would, of course, be appropriate. I don't know whether you are aware that in World War One there was more chance of a soldier becoming a psychiatric casualty than there was of him being killed by enemy fire.

It was just as bad in the Second World War. In fact, at one point psychiatric casualties were being discharged from the American Army faster than new recruits could be drafted in.

And the Falklands. The fact is that more British personnel who served in the Falklands conflict have since committed suicide since than were killed in the war itself. At least two hundred and sixty-four compared to the two hundred and fifty-five combat deaths. Same for the Argentinians. It doesn't matter which side you're on.

Nothing has changed except it's prison or Priory these days. Eddie went to the Priory. Might have been better off in prison.

They gave Eddie electric-shock treatment. It's called electroconvulsive therapy. I have to confess that I was unaware that this is still considered an appropriate treatment but apparently they use it for severe depression. Shocks it out of you, I suppose.

I should have helped him when he came to see me, when I had the chance. Before the train, before they had a go at his brain.

Scene Seven

OSCAR *is standing up holding on to the table. His wheelchair is at the other end of the table. He is trying to walk along the edge of the table to his chair. He is very slow, dragging his legs an inch at a time. He is clearly struggling.*

EDDIE *bursts into the room in a fury, surprising* OSCAR.

EDDIE. Major!

OSCAR *turns to look and falls over.*

Fuck, sorry.

EDDIE *scrambles to help* OSCAR *up.* OSCAR *is furious. He practically punches* EDDIE *who is trying to help him.* OSCAR *tries to grab him by the throat.*

OSCAR. What the hell are you doing? Are you insane? What are you doing here?

EDDIE. I had to see you.

OSCAR. These are my private quarters. You have no right to be here.

EDDIE. Well, you shouldn't live on base if you don't want people to know where you are.

EDDIE gets OSCAR back in his chair and narrowly avoids a blow to the head.

I need to speak to you.

OSCAR (*shaking with rage*). Let me be very clear, Private Clark, I would have thought you had been in the army long enough to have some idea about rank. I am a Major. I outrank you from fairly dizzying heights. Please do not let any time we have been forced to spend together to put you under a misapprehension. I am not your friend, your barrack-room buddy, I am an officer. I am not your fucking therapist. If you need to pour your ill-educated heart out then go and find someone who gives a damn. When you said you were stupid I had no idea that you were being modest.

EDDIE. I never said I was stupid. I said I had no qualifications. I want to know what this is.

EDDIE takes out a piece of paper.

OSCAR. Get me the fucking blanket.

EDDIE gets a blanket for OSCAR, who snatches it off him and puts it over his legs. EDDIE holds out the paper again.

It is a summons. You are being charged.

EDDIE. You have to let it go now.

OSCAR. Eddie, I understand that you are upset but there are procedures and they exist for a reason. We are engaged in very complex operations in an extremely uncivilised state. We cannot allow our own conduct to slip below the standards we are trying to implement. Oh, look, before the incident with the boy, you should know there had been a general investigation into Sergeant Payne's conduct.

EDDIE. Sergeant Payne was the best man in the regiment.

OSCAR. Was he really? You see, from where I stand, he seems more like a man who made the rules up as he went along.

EDDIE. He looked after us. I'm here because of Sergeant Payne.

OSCAR. Get me that file. The blue one.

EDDIE *finds the file and gives it to* OSCAR.

September the 7th. Ring any bells?

EDDIE. What?

OSCAR. September the 7th, you were on patrol with the saintly Sergeant Payne when you were alerted to a disturbance in a house. You entered and killed an unarmed man by the name of Fahran Sahar.

EDDIE. I didn't kill him.

OSCAR. Who did?

EDDIE. He was raping a woman. We saw him. He was raping a woman.

OSCAR. And you decided to kill him.

EDDIE. He was raping someone.

OSCAR. He should have been arrested. It's called 'justice'. Instead he was summarily executed.

EDDIE. It wasn't like that. It wasn't me.

OSCAR. No. It's never you, is it, Eddie? So who was it?

EDDIE *becomes tight-lipped.*

Let's see. October 1st. Ring any bells?

EDDIE. I didn't carry a fucking diary.

OSCAR. During a disturbance in the marketplace, a stallholder fell to his death down a flight of stairs.

EDDIE. I don't know what happened.

OSCAR. No one else was present at the time except Sergeant Payne and the men from his unit.

EDDIE. It was confusing.

OSCAR *removes a handgun from his briefcase.*

OSCAR. Just as confusing as when you didn't fire your gun? When you decided it was quicker to kill the boy by shoving him down a well?

EDDIE. Don't you get it? He's dead. They're all dead. It doesn't matter now. There is only me.

OSCAR. And that is a tragedy. Nevertheless, the army has a duty to make sure we know what happened. We are not in the business of covering things up. Just because we operate in lawless places does not mean we must forget the law ourselves. I'm sorry, Eddie. We have a job to do.

EDDIE. Sergeant Payne was a fucking hero.

OSCAR. To me he seems like a bloody psychopath. I have a job to do.

EDDIE. I saved your life. I pulled you from that car, Major Hadley.

OSCAR. This is not some fucking chalkboard with pluses and minuses – you can't take one life and then redeem yourself by saving another.

EDDIE. I could have left you there, you little shit. Left you to the flames where you were lying. I didn't have to save you. I don't have to save you now.

EDDIE *grabs the gun and puts it to* OSCAR*'s head.*

OSCAR. Put the gun down.

EDDIE. You don't think I should use it now? Anybody going to miss you, you little jobsworth?

OSCAR. You're crazy.

EDDIE. I am not crazy. I am angry.

OSCAR. Well, shoot me then and get it over with.

EDDIE. It's not loaded, is it?

EDDIE *throws the gun down, picks* OSCAR *up by the neck and pulls him from his wheelchair.*

OSCAR. Is this what you do now, Clark? Not enough beating up your girlfriend? Going to thrash everybody in your life? Kill the boy and now kill me?

EDDIE. You are not going to do this to my friends. You are not going to do this to me. You are not. (*Screaming.*) I was in charge. Do you understand? I was in charge.

EDDIE *lets* OSCAR *go and runs from the room.* OSCAR *falls to the floor.*

Scene Eight

EDDIE *is sitting, looking straight out. He does not move and looks vacant.*

OSCAR *wheels his chair in and looks at* EDDIE. *He moves closer to him.*

OSCAR. Hello, Eddie. My turn to visit you. Looks a comfortable place. Been on quite a ride, haven't you? Safe here though. You look fine.

Running on top of a train, they say. Must have been something. Running. Must have felt good.

Never been to one of these Priory places. God it's hot. I can hardly breathe.

They say you had a birthday. Twenty-one. Key to the door. I remember twenty-one. Thought I was a man. All grown up. Kissed my mother goodbye. My friend Phil Jackson didn't

even know where we were going on the map. At first he
thought it was somewhere near Scotland. Eight thousand
miles from home because Margaret Thatcher thought it was a
good idea. Everyone waved us off. Me and Phil, standing on
the deck. Lots of flags. My mum all tearful and proud,
sending me off to fight for some rain-sodden island that we
had never bloody heard of. 'I love you, Oscar.'

Oscar? My mother, she named me for an award.

It was chaos on the boat home. People started fighting; one
guy stabbed another guy in the stomach with a bayonet, my
legs stopped working and Thatcher got re-elected.

There is a long pause. OSCAR *gently wipes the corner of*
EDDIE*'s mouth with a handkerchief and then puts it away.*

I didn't know about the electric shock, Eddie. I would have
done something. I didn't know they still did it. Not here. I
would have tried to stop it. They'll get you back on track. I
mean, the celebrities come here. I'm so sorry.

OSCAR *starts to leave and has his back to* EDDIE *as he
starts to speak.*

EDDIE. They put wires on your head. You have to lie down and
they attach them with something sticky. It's for the tricky
patients. The ones who 'don't respond'. I didn't, didn't
respond. No point. I have nothing to say.

'I want you to draw a train that represents your life and put
the most important people in the carriages.'

There are no sodding celebrities. Just fucking rich people
moaning about their lives. Sent me to the bloody Priory. Said
I had 'stress' like I was some fucking executive who'd been
overworking. No one here from the army. Just me. No one
who knew. They put you in groups. Random groups.

'I want you to tell me about something that makes you angry.'

Tell you about something that makes me angry? Be easier to
tell you something that didn't.

And everyone was so polite and I sat and I listened. I
listened to the woman whose children didn't understand her,

to the vice-president of some shitty something-or-other who thought he should have been president and all the time I was boiling.

'The train of my life is all smashed up on the line and everyone in it is dead.' I told the group that that... That made me very angry and when I was finished no one said anything except they went to the therapist behind my back and asked for me to be moved. That I was upsetting the group. That what happened was too upsetting.

I left. I must have left.

I don't remember finding the actual train. I don't know how I got up on the roof but when they brought me back, when they were putting the electrodes on, I thought about it. I was on top of the carriage and it was moving. It was moving, it was moving and I was on the roof, on the roof, on the roof, on the roof all by myself and the wind and the noise and I were travelling, travelling so fast, the wind was whistling and for one great moment I had my arms stretched out and...

He shouts as if against the wind.

...no one was dead!

EDDIE *repeats the line almost in a whisper.*

No one was dead at all.

OSCAR *moves towards* EDDIE.

OSCAR. I brought the summons. You left it in my quarters.

He places the paper on EDDIE*'s lap and leaves.* EDDIE *looks at the paper.*

Scene Nine

OSCAR *is waiting. He sits staring out. He is tapping his hand on his wheelchair. He is agitated but trying very hard to control it.*

EDDIE *arrives and salutes.*

OSCAR. Private Clark.

EDDIE. Major.

OSCAR. How are you?

EDDIE *(stiffly)*. Not a mark on me.

OSCAR. Right. I thought it was a good idea if we went through the procedure so that you know what is going to happen. The court martial will consist of a panel of three officers. They will each have the right to ask questions and hear testimony. You will get plenty of opportunity to put your side. Do you have any questions?

EDDIE. Yes. Yes I do. Major Hadley, how is it that you are in a wheelchair?

OSCAR. I beg your pardon?

EDDIE. The wheelchair. I'm asking how you came to be in it.

OSCAR. I told you. I served in the Falklands.

EDDIE. Indeed you did. Gunner in the Royal Artillery, wasn't it? But that isn't quite the story, is it? I've been asking around.

OSCAR. I'm sure you find all of this most diverting, Private Clark, but frankly we haven't the time.

EDDIE. Haven't the time? But I'm drawing your attention to something that happened in the past. I've been reading. You should try it some time. Might surprise yourself.

I've been reading about July 20th, 1982. The Falklands War was just over. *HMS Hermes* was bringing the men home.

Yes? In fact, she was only about a day's sail away from Portsmouth Harbour and you were on board. Right? Did you or did you not have full use of your legs that morning?

OSCAR. You're not in a fit state to testify. I shall tell the Colonel.

EDDIE. You can't bear it, can you? Sergeant Payne was a fucking hero and you, you ponce, you're just a fake. 'I served in the Falklands.' Make everybody think you deserve their sympathy but you weren't injured in the war. You were on your bloody way home. You were fine. I've been checking. I've been like fucking Columbo. You remember him? Investigating. A gang of them, were there? Soldiers you served with? What did they call you when they picked you up? Ponce? Poofter? Nerd? They picked you up and dropped you down a hatch. Did you cry all the way down or hit your head and fall silently to the floor? What had you done to annoy them? You lost your legs because people couldn't stand to be with you.

OSCAR. You listen to me, you little shit, what the fuck do you know? Do you think there's some pecking order for injuries? That heroes are only made in the heat of battle, is that it? That the blokes who I served with who seem fine and then suddenly go beserk thirty years later don't count? It's because of fruitcakes like you that I am like I am. The men on the *Hermes* were drinking round the clock. I was the wrong man in the wrong place. I was unlucky. They were crazy and do you know what? I don't blame them.

We were all crazy. Ten days we waited in those trenches. Ten days, shivering, cuddling our rifles, our ears straining to see if we could hear them coming. When someone finally shouted, 'Bogies incoming!' Phil was making the tea. Tea! Making the sodding tea.

EDDIE *starts to interrupt but* OSCAR *won't have it.*

We were in charge of the missile system except we weren't really in charge because I kept telling them something was wrong but no one would listen. The system – it was supposed to protect the ships as they sailed into San Carlos Bay to land more troops but I knew that something wasn't right. I had my finger on the button. I had had my finger on the button for days. I watched as the planes came towards us. I was ready and I fired and… and nothing. The whole thing failed. The first three bombs hit the *Sir Galahad* packed with men and there was nothing I could do. Just press this fucking button… pray something was going to happen… hopeless. We left the useless thing… ran down to help… the injured. I kept calling for Phil to come and help.

Flash-fires and fireballs. Soldiers jumping in the water, clothes on fire, horrible wounds, the ground shuddering, the screams… and Phil… he got hit. He was behind me but it was chaos. I saw him but I couldn't get to him. I watched as the last shiver of life left him but he died alone and there was nothing I could do. If I had just left him making the tea, if I hadn't called… 'Phil'…

There was nothing I could do for anybody.

But no, I don't tell anyone that and I don't tell anyone how I got injured because it doesn't matter. I am not afraid of the truth. I lost the use of my legs because I went to war, that's all.

EDDIE. And I lost my mind.

OSCAR. Yes.

There is a very long pause as both men think about what they have been through. OSCAR *almost whispers when he speaks again.*

I want to help you.

EDDIE. They say I don't need help, thank you. I am discharged from the loony bin. It was 'an episode'. That's what the doctor called it. I am officially fine now. I have a medical certificate. They opened the door and off I was to go. Off to where I don't know because some fucker in a suit is 'considering' my army career. Some panel will decide my life but till then I am free to go… to go and do what? They trained me to… (*Softly.*) kill people. What shall I do with that? What do you tell people when they ask what it was like in the Falklands? Do you know my dad, my dad can't even remember whether I was in Iraq or Afghanistan?

OSCAR. You can't blame him. What's the difference to him?

EDDIE. I don't know why we're in either place.

OSCAR. There'll always be another mess, another war, and I've helped to keep that going – protocol, procedure, pathetic.

EDDIE. I'm sorry. About what I said.

OSCAR. You have nothing to be sorry about.

EDDIE. You shouldn't have called me a fruitcake.

OSCAR. No. I'm sorry.

EDDIE. What do you tell people when they ask what it was like in the Falklands?

OSCAR. I tell them it was cold and windy.

> OSCAR *cannot stop thinking about the Falklands and what happened. He looks at* EDDIE.

I'm not sure if I can do this any more. I need a drink.

> OSCAR *turns abruptly and wheels away.*

EDDIE. Major!

Scene Ten

EDDIE *is carrying* OSCAR *in to his quarters.* OSCAR *is drunk.*

EDDIE. Fucking hell. What a mess.

OSCAR. My wife left me. Said she'd rather live in the sodding Falklands.

EDDIE. When was that?

OSCAR. Ten years ago.

EDDIE. Might be time to move on. Have a tidy. Here we go.

> EDDIE *puts* OSCAR *down on the table.*

OSCAR (*laughing*). I thought you were going to punch that barman.

EDDIE. He was a cunt.

OSCAR. Private Clark, that is… that is… a fair assessment.

EDDIE. I wish I had hit him.

OSCAR. What happened at the court martial?

EDDIE. Postponed. Sat there three hours.

OSCAR. You shouldn't have been in that bar.

EDDIE. It's a pub. I needed fags. Officers only! Who did that knob think he was?

OSCAR. You didn't need to bring me home.

EDDIE. Someone had to. I'd like to punch someone.

OSCAR. Go on then. My legs might be fucked but I've a fantastic upper body.

EDDIE *punches* OSCAR *and he takes it.* EDDIE *hits him again and realises* OSCAR *will keep taking it. It is very uncomfortable.* EDDIE *stops.*

I need another drink.

EDDIE. I'll get the wheelchair.

EDDIE *goes off.*

OSCAR. I think I have a bottle of something somewhere.

EDDIE *returns, enjoying wheeling himself in the wheelchair.*

EDDIE. I bloody love this. It's great.

OSCAR. The novelty wears off after a while. In the bathroom cupboard.

EDDIE. What is?

OSCAR. Scotch.

EDDIE. The sergeant he were Scotch. Sergeant Payne. Payne by name we used to say, Payne by nature.

OSCAR. Scott*ish*.

EDDIE. What?

OSCAR. He was Scottish. The drink is Scotch.

EDDIE. If the drink were *in* him would it be Scottish?

OSCAR. You are education's loss.

EDDIE. I don't suppose it matters now.

OSCAR. Bathroom cabinet.

EDDIE. Yes, sir.

EDDIE *wheels off to get the bottle.*

OSCAR. Did you ever find out what Burnley means?

EDDIE (*off*). Yes.

OSCAR. What?

EDDIE (*off*). It means 'shithole'.

Not used to the wheelchair, we hear him crash into something.

Ow, fuck!

OSCAR. Mind how you go.

EDDIE *returns with the bottle and a tooth mug. He pours out some Scotch for* OSCAR.

EDDIE. That's what my granddad used to say. Mind how you go. I think he should have been clearer. The place is mined, mind how you go. Mind your mind when you go. Your mind may go if you are mined. Not everything means something, you know, Major? Sometimes things are meaningless. I'd better go.

OSCAR. Have a drink.

EDDIE. I don't think so. Won't you get into trouble?

OSCAR. I have read a report which categorically states that 'Within British military culture alcohol is seen as "aiding social interaction and unit cohesion".' Drinking with you is practically a duty which I fulfil despite being appalled by it.

EDDIE (*looking at the bottle of Scotch*). I don't really drink. Left that to me dad. Scared if I start I'll never stop.

OSCAR. Not a problem. We'll put you in the Priory. To the regiment.

OSCAR *clinks his cup against the bottle and* EDDIE *reluctantly takes a sip from the bottle.*

EDDIE. Down the hatch!

OSCAR. Very funny. Oh, good boy. Why did you join up, Eddie?

EDDIE. Nothing else to do. Everyone I knew worked at mill, weaving, but that's all gone now. Gone to China. Nothing my dad didn't know about the looms. Been on shop floor all his life. I bet he could have gone to China an' all. Nice job but he don't like Chinese food. Gives him wind. I said he should go. Have an adventure.

OSCAR. I'd like a Chinese adventure. Did you want an adventure?

EDDIE. Used to. Now all I want is to climb up Pendle Hill. It's near us. It's all I think about. Where I go in my head. I used to tell the others about Pendle. Jack laughed – said I were 'away with the hills'. It's Irish. Irish for crazy. Away with the hills. Did you know he was Irish? Jack was Irish. Jack. He was crazy. Not as crazy as Harley. Listened to his iPod the whole time. Taking orders, Harley's on the iPod. Being shot at – Harley's on the iPod.

OSCAR. Why?

EDDIE. Didn't like the sound of guns. Jack from Ireland, Harley from Wales and Paki, Paki, I don't know... London. Brian was a bastard Brummie. Sergeant Payne he was from... Glasgow. Do you want to see a Glasgow kiss?

EDDIE *pretends to headbutt* OSCAR. *Suddenly he feels awkward.*

Just kidding. I shouldn't be here.

OSCAR. You are a philosopher! An existentialist question – where should we be?

EDDIE. You been to Lancashire?

OSCAR. That is something in a long list of things I can't remember.

EDDIE. You'd know. Rains all the fucking time. My gran used to say, 'If you can see Pendle then it's about to rain, if you can't then it's already started.'

OSCAR. Pendle, pen-del, Pendle. There's a hill. Is it a big hill?

EDDIE. Big enough. Steep. Lots of rocks. Brings out a sweat when you climb. Worth it, though. Get to the top, your heart pounding like a jackhammer and you look out...

OSCAR. What do you see?

EDDIE. Green. It's all green and... I don't know. The wind and the rain try to knock you back down again but you don't let it. You stand there and you know you're... (*Shrugging*.) Alive. You'd like it with your history books and all. There's a... what you call it... an old burial site at the top. Granddad told me. Bronze Age, I think. I don't know. He liked history, Granddad.

OSCAR. They must have thought a lot of their dead to take them all the way up there. Carrying them up the hill.

EDDIE. I never thought of that. Nice view for them. Nice place to say goodbye. Carry them up in your arms. Feel the sweat running down your back. Hold them tight till you lay them down safe at the top.

OSCAR. How high did you say it was?

EDDIE. I told you. High, you fucker, and green. Bloody green and I love it. I'm tired of the dust.

OSCAR. Khaki. It's Persian for 'dust'.

EDDIE. I don't think I'll ever mind the rain again.

OSCAR. You know what, you had a very foolish teacher. You do just fine with words.

EDDIE *picks up an iPod from the table and starts scrolling through it.*

EDDIE. What music do you have?

OSCAR. Nothing you'd like.

EDDIE. Why, is it all la-di-da? All violins and nothing to hum along to? Fat women singing foreign? What have you got on here?

OSCAR. I have some… pop… music.

EDDIE. *Pop* music? Ooh, you trendsetter. Let me see.

EDDIE *goes to have a look.*

Kool and the Gang? Kool with a K, how cool is that?

OSCAR. Kool and the Gang were very big… in the eighties.

EDDIE. Pop music, Major Hadley, is supposed to be *pop*ular.

OSCAR. There's some current stuff.

EDDIE. Oh yes, Hot Chocolate. Are these in temperature order?

OSCAR. I have eclectic taste.

EDDIE. What did you used to dance to? You like dancing.

OSCAR. How do you know that?

EDDIE. In the hospital, you told me.

OSCAR. I don't remember.

EDDIE. How is your mum?

OSCAR. My mother? She passed away years ago. My friend Phil, he called out for his mother.

EDDIE. Right. What did your dad reckon to you dancing?

OSCAR. He hated it. My bloody father. Teased me till I joined the fucking army – make a man of me.

EDDIE. Made half a man of you. (*Starts to laugh and stops.*) Sorry.

OSCAR (*laughing*). Half a bloody man.

EDDIE. Anyway, I didn't mean anything. I wouldn't mind dancing meself. Like the old films. I wouldn't mind that.

EDDIE *pretends to dance.* OSCAR *suddenly has a thought.*

OSCAR. Ah! William Rimmer!

EDDIE. Rimmer? Sounds disgusting.

OSCAR. William Rimmer. Best brass-band music of all time. He was from Lancashire. Must be in your bloody DNA.

EDDIE. Oh aye. Brass bands. It's all we live for 'oop north'. We listen to brass bands while wearing clogs and feeding whippets pie and peas in the rain while we wait for our homing pigeons to return with news of our missing flat caps.

OSCAR *puts on William Rimmer's 'Honour the Brave' and* EDDIE *can't help but start marching and pretending he is leading a parade. He is like a boy playing at soldiers.* OSCAR *laughs and joins in dancing around* EDDIE *in his wheelchair. They have a wonderful time. Carried away,* OSCAR *decides to try and stand. He gets up from the wheelchair and crumples to the floor. As he does so he makes a terrible sound of utter despair that is almost animal-like.* EDDIE *notices. He stops the music and is uncertain what to do. He hovers over* OSCAR, *unable to touch him.*

Major, don't do this. I need you to not do this. Stop it. You have to stop.

Major, please don't do this. Please.

Scene Eleven

OSCAR *is trying to pull himself together from the night before. The radio is playing.*

NEWSREADER (*voice-over*). Two hundred thousand people are now said to have fled Syria's largest city, Aleppo, following days of clashes between rebels and the military. Refugees described the city as being besieged by government troops and beset by incessant shelling. Food supplies and petrol are running low and black-market prices for everyday staples are soaring.

OSCAR turns off the radio. EDDIE brings in a cup of tea.
OSCAR is embarrassed.

EDDIE. Two sugars.

OSCAR. Thank you.

EDDIE. Anything else I can do for you, Major?

OSCAR. No, thank you, Clark, I'm fine. Absolutely fine.

EDDIE. What happens now about the court martial?

OSCAR. You'll be notified.

EDDIE. I'm off then.

OSCAR. Splendid.

EDDIE leaves OSCAR sitting with his tea. After a moment,
OSCAR picks up his iPhone and begins to dictate into it.

In my professional experience, I do not believe that further
investigation into this matter… I do not believe that given
the circumstances, further investigation into this matter…
My own experience suggests… that Private Edward Clark…
Eddie.

The lights fade. Passage of time.

Scene Twelve

OSCAR is in his quarters. He looks exhausted. There is a knock
at the door. OSCAR hears it but does not answer. EDDIE
enters.

EDDIE. You didn't answer. Did you not hear?

OSCAR. I'm busy.

EDDIE. No one's seen you for a week. They said you've not
been well.

OSCAR. I'm fine. I'm busy.

EDDIE. Is it your ears again?

OSCAR. I would really appreciate it if you would bugger off,
Clark. I have nothing to say to you. Just leave me alone. I'm
going to make sure they drop the case. Did you hear what I
said?

EDDIE. That's not why I came. I've an invite for you.

EDDIE *puts down an invitation.*

OSCAR. Suzanne forgiven you?

EDDIE. What?

OSCAR. You getting married? The invite.

EDDIE. No. It's from me dad. You met him at the airbase. He's
having a ceremony. Wants you to come.

OSCAR. What kind of ceremony?

EDDIE. For the lads. A plaque. In the church. In Burnley.
They're not even from round there. My dad's not been in that
sodding church since he got married. Suddenly we all have
to go and the vicar's coming round to discuss it. I said I'd
ask. He wants some brass there.

OSCAR. Thank you.

EDDIE. It's a long way. It's just a plaque. You don't… And this.

EDDIE *pulls out another piece of paper.*

OSCAR. What's that?

EDDIE. A statement. I want to make a statement about what
happened. About me killing the boy. I want to confess.

OSCAR. Why now, Eddie?

EDDIE. There's a bloke. From the papers…

OSCAR. A journalist?

EDDIE. Yeah. From the papers in London. He's asking
questions about the lads. I want it sorted. I don't want any
more questions. They were heroes. They were fucking heroes.

EDDIE *leaves.* OSCAR *stares at the piece of paper.*

Scene Thirteen

EDDIE *is in the church.* OSCAR *enters in his chair.*

EDDIE. I didn't think you'd come.

OSCAR. Your dad asked me. I did know them.

EDDIE. He asked everyone, the whole fucking town was here.

OSCAR. The plaque looks good.

EDDIE. Fucking plaque. Should have had a party. A big, noisy, fucking party. With singing and dancing. Not some boring fart in a church. Going on about a piece of wood with their names on.

OSCAR. I used to think it was enough – plaques and medals; marching bands and speeches from dull people who stayed at home but were with us all the way and that way we all know that what we did was necessary, just and righteous. The families seemed pleased. At least it was good for them. I talked to Jack's father, Brian's mother… how long's it been?

EDDIE. Four months. Hakim's sister asked me what it was like out there.

OSCAR. What did you say?

EDDIE. I said it were hot and dusty.

OSCAR. Your dad did a good thing. Your friends died. People find it difficult. They're awkward. He was trying to show you today. Your father is very proud of you.

EDDIE. Yes he is. Did you hear him? Kept telling his mates. 'Our Eddie's been in the Priory with them celebrities. We couldn't believe it when we heard. Didn't just send him anywhere. They looked after him, the army did. He looks good, doesn't he, Eddie? Not a mark on him. Not one. We were so relieved, his mum and me.' As if he ever notices my mum.

EDDIE *pulls a small bag from his pocket.*

Sausage roll?

OSCAR *declines but smiles.*

OSCAR. Suzanne? The sausage rolls?

EDDIE. Probably. She doesn't really speak to me now. Mum and Dad see her. I know they think of her as family. More than me. She wanted to get engaged. I couldn't. Engage, that's something we do with the enemy. I said I'm sorry.

EDDIE *looks at the sausage rolls and puts them back in his pocket.*

OSCAR. Your father asked me what we had been fighting for.

EDDIE. What did you tell him?

OSCAR. I said that I wasn't sure because…

OSCAR *rattles off a very fast analysis.*

…although the lid had been taken off the pressure cooker of dictatorship that still left a vacuum of political belief and that the imposition of a western model of democracy was unlikely to work. I explained that none of the other countries in that region with despotic rulers want us to succeed and that the most the West can strive for is a stabilisation of the region with a future financial incentive to realise the vast potential mineral wealth.

EDDIE. Did you really?

OSCAR. No. I said we were fighting for freedom.

EDDIE. Sounds good.

OSCAR. He nodded and said he knew that Saddam was a bad man. That he knew he'd killed a million people. I didn't tell him how many have died on our watch. That we are just there to make the politicians look good. Look at Blair, he got great ratings, especially in America. The spoils of war.

EDDIE. You got that cool chair. Makes everyone love you. That woman from the charity couldn't get enough of you.

OSCAR. She wanted to persuade me to run the marathon.

EDDIE. Why don't you? Nothing people like better than a legless git having a go. Makes them buy poppies. Not like those of us who've just been a bit loopy. We don't raise that much money.

OSCAR. I don't know, I think you'd look great on a poster. Electrodes on your head, dribble dripping down your chin. Might have trouble getting the picture. You do shake a bit.

OSCAR *takes a piece of paper out of his pocket and hands it to* EDDIE.

Take this. It's your confession. I didn't hand it in.

EDDIE. What is your fucking problem? You chase me when I'm in the fucking loony bin and suddenly it's all okay?

OSCAR. I didn't believe you.

EDDIE. What do you want me to say? I killed a boy. I picked him up. What else? He had a shirt, a baggy shirt and I tore it and I could feel his skin under my hands. He was eight years old. I threw him down a well and murdered him. You should be worrying about him not me. Harley were crying and the sarge was moaning but I heard the splash. Maybe I could still have saved him then but I didn't. He saw his mum die. He must have seen his mum die. Maybe he thought I would help him.

OSCAR. Why are you doing this? Because you are alive and the others are not? Is that it? Trying to salve your conscience?

EDDIE. Oh, fuck off! I didn't want to say goodbye to the lads like this.

OSCAR. Shall we go and do it properly?

'Honour the Brave' begins to play quietly.

Scene Fourteen

EDDIE *has been pushing* OSCAR *up Pendle Hill. He carries a small rucksack.*

EDDIE. What were that music called again?

OSCAR. 'Honour the Brave.'

> EDDIE *carries on.*

Look, I've changed my mind. It's fucking freezing.

EDDIE. Welcome to Lancashire. You'll be fine. Come on. No more path left now.

> EDDIE *moves to pick* OSCAR *up out of his chair.*

OSCAR. We should have come up in the car.

EDDIE. The Bronze Age warrior did not have a bloody car. You have to climb Pendle Hill. On foot. That's the whole point.

OSCAR. But I am not climbing.

EDDIE. That is because you are an officer and therefore officially, a lazy bastard.

OSCAR. Ha bloody ha. Is it much further?

EDDIE. We're here, look!

> EDDIE *puts* OSCAR *down and turns the music off.*

OSCAR. It's so green.

EDDIE. Told you.

OSCAR. It's beautiful.

EDDIE. Yes.

> EDDIE *takes out a bottle of cheap cider and has a swig before passing it to* OSCAR.

OSCAR. I looked it up. Burnley – it used to be Brun Lea – it means valley by the River Brun but that's not the best. Pendle Hill – Pendle is from a Cumbric word, that's a kind of Celtic that used to be spoken in the north, Pen means 'hill' and so does 'dle'. They added the hill part when people forgot what Pendle meant.

EDDIE. So Pendle Hill just means Hill Hill Hill?

OSCAR. Delightful, isn't it?

EDDIE. Bloody typical.

OSCAR. History, you see, Eddie, people should pay attention.

EDDIE. It don't matter now.

OSCAR. No.

EDDIE. D'you know what?

OSCAR. What?

EDDIE. All I wanted today was to be up there with them. On the plaque. Till I saw their names I didn't know I was the one who was missing. Sergeant David Payne, Privates Harley Jones, Hakim Kuok, Jack McNeil and Brian Robinson. They'll be on that wall for ever now. Together.

OSCAR. Eddie, I need to tell you something. I lied.

EDDIE. You lied?

OSCAR. I lied about what the others said. No one had said a word. Jack, Hakim, Brian. No one said anything about you or the boy.

EDDIE. No one?

OSCAR. No.

EDDIE. Why would you lie about that?

OSCAR. To get you to talk. I couldn't have guessed they would die.

EDDIE *begins laughing*.

What's funny? There's nothing funny.

EDDIE. You. Is this you trying to make it all better now?

OSCAR. Isn't that what you were doing with your confession?

EDDIE. I'm going to 'Honour the Brave'. The lads and I didn't finish the job. I want to go back. I want to be redeployed.

OSCAR. They won't let you.

EDDIE. I have to finish the job. That's all I keep thinking. I couldn't sleep with Suzanne because I couldn't sleep. In my head I kept going through the villages and there were bodies by the side of the road and bits of people lying there. Driving through villages where people were dead and the buildings were crumbling around them. And the smell. The butcher-house smell of shit, blood, burned flesh and rotting decay... It can't have been for nothing. I owe them.

OSCAR. Eddie, they won't send you back now.

EDDIE. Maybe.

OSCAR. Look, let's just say goodbye to the lads.

EDDIE. I brought some music.

OSCAR. Not more bloody marching?

EDDIE. No.

> EDDIE *puts on the music. It is Kool and the Gang singing 'Celebration'.*

OSCAR. Kool and the Gang?

EDDIE. They were very big in the eighties.

> EDDIE *gets to his feet.*

Shall we dance?

OSCAR. Yes.

> EDDIE *picks* OSCAR *up and dances joyously.*

Epilogue

OSCAR. I want to stand for this bit. I want to stand up.

OSCAR *tries to stand and shakily does so.*

I have something to read – 'It was with deep regret that the formal investigation into the death of the boy known simply as Omar, concluded that while the army were almost certainly responsible for the child's demise it was not possible to identify the individual soldier responsible. A formal statement of regret will be issued in due course.'

Tragically, the death of this boy was not an isolated incident. If you put young men, any young men in a strange place, deprive them of sleep, frighten them and let things happen that change their fear to hate, then no one should be surprised at the outcome. Yet we expect these young men to have nobility when we probably wouldn't have it ourselves.

Private Edward Clark was refused permission to be redeployed and was given an honourable discharge. That same morning, when he was told, he took his own life. It was the only time he ever fired a gun at anyone.

The End.